TRAVELING WITH THE TIDE

An Experience of a Lifetime

By Dr. Christopher L. Bramlett

Compiled by Lewis P. Bramlett

My father worked at the University of Alabama from 1967 to 1977. Even though he did not attend the school as a student, he became a big fan of the football program and still is to this day. He has a unique perspective of the football team having been given the opportunity to travel with them for several games.

For a number of years my father has been a member of several message boards for University of Alabama sports fans. The information in this booklet, that he shared on one of the message boards, is his description of those experiences traveling with the team.

Lewis P. Bramlett

TABLE OF CONTENTS

INTRODUCTION

Chris and Pat Bramlett along with kids Lewis, John and Susan – 1970's

Following my post about having traveled with the team during the Bear Bryant years, a number of you asked that I expand on those experiences. In order to keep the individual posts to a reasonable length, I will segment the trips into several episodes, each dealing with a different aspect. Please understand that the time to which we are referring was quite a long time ago (30+ years) so do not expect my memory to be as sharp as it used to be. For that reason, I plan to include only those events about which I can be reasonably certain. Furthermore, I cannot even be certain as to which occurrence went with which trip. I am sure you will understand if the chronology is not exact.

The travel to which I will be referring took place sometime during the years 1969- 1973. I had joined the faculty of the Chemistry Department in 1967 and left the University in 1977. However, the last four of those years I was serving as Associate Dean of the Graduate School and Assistant Vice President for Research. Since I was not dealing with undergraduates during that period, I am sure that the invitations came prior to that time. I had my closest association during the period 1970-1973 when I was serving as Assistant Dean of the College of Arts and Sciences. I handled student academic affairs and had quite a lot of contact with Coach Bryant's assistant who dealt with the player's academic programs.

Clark Hall
Offices of the College of Arts and Sciences

At this point it would be informative to say something about academics and football during those years. First, as a Chemistry professor I taught many football players, and I can tell you that many of Coach Bryant's players are now physicians, attorneys, engineers, business leaders and other successful people throughout the state and, indeed, the nation. Most of the players who took my chemistry class were the kinds of young men you wanted your boys to be like when they grew up. I can also tell you that as professor and dean, I was never asked for any special consideration for a player. The only accommodation I can recall having been accorded members of the football team was that during fall

Coach Paul "Bear" Bryant

registration they were allowed to register first. That made it possible for them to schedule labs and other afternoon classes so as not to interfere with practice. A day or so after registration the academic advisor was in my office getting copies of class schedules so that he could arrange for the study halls and tutorials that were commonplace for the time.

Coach Bryant had the policy of inviting four faculty members to each game. I have no idea how they were chosen, but I can guess that the chosen professors were those who had quite a bit of contact with the players. I do know that prior to an invitation's being rendered, I was called by the academic advisor to make sure I would be able to travel with the team on the weekend in question. Once the date was cleared, a day or so later I received a personal letter from Coach Bryant issuing the formal invitation to travel with the team for the given game. Unfortunately, I did not keep all of those letters. I did, however, keep one of them. My son had that letter framed, and it hangs in a prominent place in his house to this day.

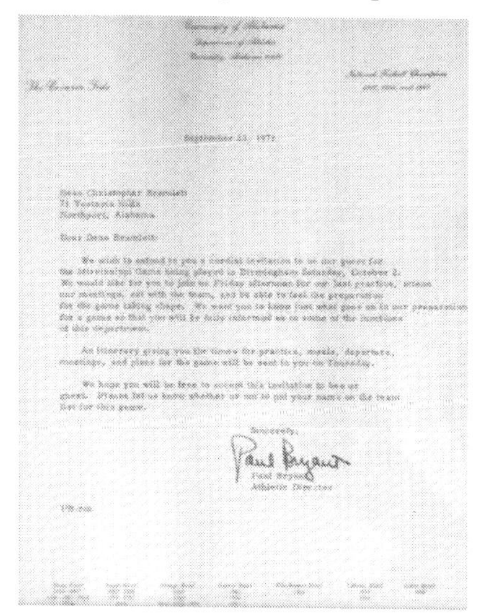

Sincerely,

Paul Bryant
Athletic Director

Invitation letter from Coach Bryant's office to the October 2, 1971 game against Ole Miss

FRIDAY'S TEAM MEETING

We were instructed to meet the team at the athletic dormitory at noon for lunch on Friday before Saturday's game. You have probably heard many tales about the fine food that was served the players, and I can tell you they are all true. The food served at that lunch would have graced some of the finest restaurants in Alabama. In addition, I believe it was the practice that any player could order a strip steak, cooked to his requirement, at any meal, including breakfast.

Following the meal, we boarded the buses for the short hop over to Coach Bryant's offices in the coliseum.

Coleman Coliseum

At this point, two things struck me. First, the players were all dressed handsomely in their crimson blazers and neat haircuts, and they were extremely deferential to the faculty members traveling with them. They all looked as though they were on their way to church. Second, they were quiet as church mice. Hardly a word was spoken from this point on. Later, I could only guess that this was part of the "psyching" ritual that got the men totally focused on next day's game.

We left the buses and were ushered into the building and into a small amphitheater that looked like it might have seated 150 or so. In attendance were the players, assistant coaches and faculty members. After we were seated, there was a deathly silence throughout the room. I mean silence. Not a word was spoken. This went on for several minutes after which a door opened and in came the Bear. He walked into the room without saying a word and took a position front and center. He had some sort of paper rolled up in his fist, and he kept hitting that roll in the palm of his other hand. He just stood there. After what seemed like an eternity, he walked slowly over to the player seated in the front row to his right and took a position directly in front of him. He stopped with the rolled-up paper, looked straight down into the eyes of the poor player in front of him and just stared at him. After what seemed like another eternity, he slowly walked to the player seating next and repeated the staring. Then the next, and the next, until he had stared down every player on that first row.

After this ritual, Coach Bryant went back to front and center, and said something that has stuck with me to this day. He said, in that gravely voice of his, "Men, don't ever let them surprise you." After a pause he elaborated on what he meant. And the meaning was quite clear.

I do not remember what else might have been said, but I believe there was some talk about which assistant coach was in charge of the game.

TRAVELING TO LEGION FIELD

Mary Harmon Bryant

Following the team meeting in the coliseum, we boarded the buses for Birmingham. Here another tradition prevailed. The Bear always sat by himself in the right-hand seat of the first bus. Nobody would have dared sit with him. Even his wife, Mary Harmon, rode on a different bus. I usually sat with her as I knew some of her family members who went to our church.

At this point the public got involved. As we were leaving Tuscaloosa, a lot of people would stand at street-side to watch the buses go by. A lot of "Roll Tides" were rendered by bystanders. I recall one hilarious event. As we passed by a beauty parlor, all of a sudden, some lady came running out the front door, still wrapped in some sort of cape with hair in various stages of dishevelment, and headed toward us yelling "Roll Tide" at the top of her voice.

The ride through Tuscaloosa was slow then rapid to Bessemer. During those years the Tide stayed at the Holiday Inn in Bessemer. It was weird! The entire time we were there, there was hardly a car in sight as the team rented every room. Police kept everyone else out.

As we disembarked, our host (academic advisor) gave us our room key and told us to meet back at the buses at 4:00 for the trip to Legion Field for a short workout. Well, on the first trip old dummy here did not make it back to the buses at exactly 4:00. I suppose I was not yet indoctrinated to the Bear's penchant for punctuality. I quickly learned that the buses had left at exactly 4:00 p.m. and there I was, all alone, in that huge motel. Well, almost alone. There was a lone Highway Patrolman stationed where the buses had been parked. When he spotted me, he asked if I were Dr. Bramlett. I replied, "Yes, and I am terribly embarrassed." He told me to hop in his cruiser and he proceeded to take me to Legion field. I am telling you, blue lights and siren were going full blast. On arrival at Legion field I sheepishly found my way to the other faculty members and vowed never to make that same mistake again.

On another trip I took with the team, I very definitely made it back to the buses by 4:00 and traveled with them to the stadium. Here, another great tradition came to light. I soon found out why the team was so dead set on leaving at exactly 4:00 p.m. You see, the people of Bessemer and the stadium section of Birmingham knew exactly when the team was to come by on its way to the stadium, and they lined the streets screaming "Roll Tide" at the tops of their voices as we traveled by.

The Friday workout was usually short and in shoulder pads and shorts. On one occasion I was puzzled by what some of the players were doing. They were behaving like children. They were batting the ball around and diving for it to see if they could catch it before it hit the ground. Looked sort of silly. The next day I found out why they were doing that drill. The opponent was LSU, and the quarterback was Bert Jones. Remember him? Well, Bert Jones threw the ball so hard that often the receiver simply could not hold on to it, or it hit him in the pads and bounced off. Alabama intercepted a number of his passes by diving for the ball after it had bounced off the receiver.

Just in case I don't get around to saying this later on, I want to add here that one cannot imagine the degree of organization and preparation the team went through prior to the game. The Bear was undoubtedly a great coach. But, he was an even better organizer and motivator.

FRIDAY NIGHT

After returning from the Friday afternoon workout at Legion Field we had an absolutely wonderful dinner at the motel. After dinner I believe the assistant in charge of the game had a few words after which we all went to a movie.

Let me now say a few words about assistants' being in charge of a game. As I observed things, it seemed as though one assistant coach was assigned to develop the game plan for each game. He was in charge of scouting and making the assignments, etc. It may be that that is the way it is always done, but at the time it seemed somewhat innovative. One fallout from this was that the assistant coaches were well prepared to become head coaches. As I recall most of the assistants at that time did go on to become head coaches and/or athletic directors.

John Croyle

I remember nothing about the movie. However, after it was over, we returned to the motel where ice cream sandwiches and milk were awaiting the team. I do recall that I saw John Croyle head for his room with his arm totally stacked with cartons of milk and ice cream sandwiches.

After that it was lights out.

GAME DAY MORNING

Saturday morning, there was no formal meal until about 10:00 a.m. or so. Since a lot of us were accustomed to rising much earlier than that, I found my way down to the motel café where the assistant coaches were gathered for coffee. It was delightful sitting there for well over an hour just listening to the coaches talk about all sorts of things, including recruiting, today's game etc. I can only name a few of the assistants at the time but some of them were Mal Moore, Dude Hennessey, Jack Rutledge, Bill Oliver, Pat Dye and John David Crow. They were all very cordial to us and included us in the conversation.

Mal Moore | **Dude Hennessey** | **Jack Rutledge**

After the coffee time we all went back to our rooms to dress for the game. As I mentioned above, the pre-game meal was sometime around 10:00 a.m. The meal was very simple-steak, toast and iced tea. That's all! After the meal came one of the most memorable events in my memory. Of course, each meal included a prayer delivered by one of the team members or assistant coaches. At the conclusion of the meal, and this was a ritual followed every time I was with them, Coach Bryant would stand up, make a few comments about the day's game, then turn the meeting over to the assistant coach in charge. I will paraphrase as best I can, "Coach------ will now take over the meeting, while I take a walk with my quarterback." At that point the assistant in charge would talk for a few minutes (no one ever spoke for a long time) and you would see Coach Bryant and the starting quarterback leave the room, going gosh knows where to discuss gosh knows what.

After the meal it was just about time to get on the bus for the ride to Legion Field and the game.

GAME DAY

You can imagine how exciting it was for a young faculty member to arrive at the stadium with the Crimson Tide and its fabled "Bear." There were huge crowds waiting at the gates as the buses pulled in. Again, the players were extremely quiet and dressed like they were going to church. From the buses we walked, in street clothes, out onto the field I suppose just to get the "feel" of things. As early as it was, the student section was already filling up, if not filled. There were very few other fans in the stadium at that time.

I will never forget this. Every game I traveled with the team, the Bear would walk around the field for a while then stroll over to the student section where he would wave and doff his hound's-tooth hat several times. The students would go absolutely berserk. After that he would assume his pose at the goal posts for the last few minutes of the walk-around.

When we got back into the dressing room, the players began dressing and the ankle taping was finished. That in itself was a pageant worthy of addressing, but I will spare you that this go-around. While that was going on, we were invited into a separate room where Coach Bryant had his pre-game meeting with the assistant coaches. That was incredible. I can still see Coach Bryant donning his long johns and heavy shoes, at the same time talking non-stop to the assistants, going over numerous details of who was to play when and where and under what circumstances. His memory and control of the situation was so different than his Sunday telecasts when he often appeared to know less than Charley Thornton. I can tell you that was all a façade.

Coach Bryant was always in charge of his wits and the situation. In fact, while he was speaking, many of the assistants were still taking notes.

When all was in readiness, the assistant in charge made a few comments while "scouts" kept track of when the appropriate time would be to come out of the "tunnel." I can remember none of the details of our going through the tunnel. I do recall that the team ran, and we walked. I also recall a few yells of recognition from some of my students who happened to be sitting in the sections close enough for us to be recognized.

One thing impressed me greatly about being on the bench so close to the action. Those running backs take off like rockets. I know they always appeared fast on television and from the stands, but nothing like I saw up close. Even in the pre-game warm-up they were like lightning.

Let me make another point about preparation. At one of the games, Alabama kicked off using an on-sides kick, recovering the ball and going on in to score. Let me remind you. I was with the team and coaches from the time we got on the bus Friday at noon until the game was over and we were back in Tuscaloosa. I heard every speech. But I had no idea they were going to use the on-sides kick. That is an indication of how programmed and prepared the team was for the game.

Halftime: Over the years many of my friends have asked me what the Coach would tell the team at halftime. They were especially inquisitive about an Ole Miss game in which the score was 13-6 at half, and the Tide ended up 42-6. What could he have told the team to get them so motivated? To be honest, there was never any

Coach Bryant at halftime

hoop-la during the halftime break. It was very clinical. Each assistant worked with his players using a lot of X's and O's. Again, my impression was Coach Bryant relied more on preparation than emotion.

I can also relate one anecdote about an incident during halftime. Do you remember Terry Davis? To me Terry Davis was the quintessential wishbone quarterback. In fact, I think he was not only the first, but the best wishbone quarterback Alabama ever had. In any case, I recall one game in which Terry Davis came into the dressing room, took off his shoulder pads, and leaned against the wall, totally beat up. You remember, the wishbone quarterback got tackled every play. And, on this particular day, Terry had been beaten to a pulp. I saw the Bear finish crushing him. I was close enough to hear the Bear tell Terry, "If that excessive talking in the huddle doesn't stop, I will have me a new quarterback." Although Terry was crushed, it was temporary as he went out and demolished the opponent.

Terry Davis

The post-game was also the same. Fortunately, I never saw them lose. Shortly before the end, the academic advisor would gather up the faculty and take us into the dressing room. I am sure he did that because once the team started for the dressing room, we might have gotten run over had we been en route. Then came another surprise. Instead of coming into the dressing room whooping and hollering, the players filed in, still quiet as church mice, and knelt in silent prayer. You could hear a pin drop. Then the Bear would say "amen" and all hell would break loose.

The ride back to Tuscaloosa was totally different than the ride up. It was a time for catharsis! The players were jubilant and riotous. However, they still reacted to us with the greatest of decorum.

And that's the story. I suppose you can now understand how a guy who was a graduate of two of the biggest losers in football history, Wake Forest (BS 1960 and MS 1964) and the University of Virginia (Ph.D. Chemistry 1967), became one of the most ardent supports of the Crimson Tide. Both of those schools set national records for losing streaks while I was in school.

"ROLL TIDE"

~~

Program cover for game attended that matches the letter/invitation shown earlier.

Pictures below are from one of a number of return trips to Tuscaloosa and the University of Alabama that we have made since moving away. These buildings, along with the Chemistry building, were where I spent much of my time.

Clark Hall

Rose Administration Building

"No coach has ever won a game by what he knows; it's what his players know that counts."

"Show class, have pride, and display character. If you do, winning takes care of itself."

"If anything goes bad, I did it. If anything goes semi-good, we did it. If anything goes really good, then you did it. That's all it takes to get people to win football games for you.

Coach Paul "Bear" Bryant

Made in the USA
Middletown, DE
09 September 2023